Mountain Streams

Mountain Streams

Restoring Our Nature

THOMAS NISBETT

RESOURCE *Publications* • Eugene, Oregon

MOUNTAIN STREAMS
Restoring Our Nature

Copyright © 2025 Thomas Nisbett. All rights reserved. Except for brief quotations in critical publications or reviews, no part of this book may be reproduced in any manner without prior written permission from the publisher. Write: Permissions, Wipf and Stock Publishers, 199 W. 8th Ave., Suite 3, Eugene, OR 97401.

Resource Publications
An Imprint of Wipf and Stock Publishers
199 W. 8th Ave., Suite 3
Eugene, OR 97401

www.wipfandstock.com

PAPERBACK ISBN: 979-8-3852-5361-6
HARDCOVER ISBN: 979-8-3852-5362-3
EBOOK ISBN: 979-8-3852-5363-0

08/11/25

Unless otherwise indicated, all Scripture quotations are taken from *THE MESSAGE*, copyright © 1993, 2002, 2018 by Eugene H. Peterson. Used by permission of NavPress. All rights reserved. Represented by Tyndale House Publishers, Inc.

Scripture quotations marked (NASB) taken from the (NASB®) New American Standard Bible®, Copyright © 1960, 1971, 1977, 1995 by The Lockman Foundation. Used by permission. All rights reserved. lockman.org

"There are not many people who have experienced mountain streams all over the world and in more unique settings than Tom Nisbett. Tom is also deeply immersed in the writings and life of E. Stanley Jones, one of the great contextual Christian leaders of the last century who is not widely known in the West. That combination of experiences and reflection invites us to a refreshing and wise collection of engagements that provide insight into creation, the creator, and provides nourishment for the soul. This is a perfect pocket companion for the next hiking trip, time at the lake, afternoon on the porch, or for the time when you need to escape to a place where you can find rest, inspiration, and refreshment."

—**Steve G.W. Moore,** CEO Emeritus, M. J. Murdock Trust

"What a delightful book! It is so easy to read, so engaging, and so full of wisdom. Tom, who I have hiked with on the North Shore mountains, makes the mountains come alive. He helps you see them with fresh eyes, seeing God's glory shining through. His references to fellow mentor Dr. E. Stanley Jones showed a deep appreciation of the gift of God's creation, how the world is designed to work in Christ's way. His weaving of the physical and spiritual is done seamlessly. I highly commend this book to others."

—**Ed Hird,** Group of Four,
International United Christian Ashram

"It's a delight to follow Tom Nisbett's spiritual streams of consciousness from the his beloved mountains to the living waters that nurture us all. He reminds us that 'The Lamb at the heart of the throne will be our shepherd and will lead us to streams of life-giving water. He will wipe every tear from our eyes' (Rev 7:17)."

—**Donna Bell Sanders,** Mission Coordinator,
United Christian Ashrams International

"*Mountain Streams* offers a gentle, steady flow of devotionals where ecology and faith meet in everyday experience. Drawing inspiration from missionary E. Stanley Jones and naturalist Aldo Leopold, Thomas Nisbett invites readers to reflect on both their inner nature and the natural world, encouraging a deeper, more attentive walk with God. This is a thoughtful companion for anyone seeking spiritual renewal rooted in creation."

—**Don Gordon,** CEO,
C3-Christians Caring for Creation

"*Mountain Streams* by Tom Nisbett is a moving book about our spirituality and nature. It is a reminder we are intertwined with creation, needing to allow ourselves to be present in and care for the beauty around us. While I myself am not a hiker or climber, the powerful descriptive words of Tom led me straight to the mountain top or sitting next to the gurgling stream. I was reminded how healing it is to be in nature, especially upon a wooded trail or looking across a mountain vista. God speaks to us when we quiet our minds and spirit, join him in his creation. Don't miss this opportunity to be transported to a place of deep meaning and connection."

—**Shana Chaplin,** Chief Program Officer,
Winthrop Rockefeller Institute

Contents

1. From the Source | 1
2. The Eli Stanley Jones Stream | 4
   A Journey of Faith and Belief
3. The Aldo Leopold Stream | 8
   Exploring the Earth and Its Stewardship
4. Reflections | 12

BROOKS

    Restoration | 17
    Receptivity | 19
    Mystery | 21
    Eternity | 23
    Early | 25
    Refill | 27
    Rhythm | 29
    Exploring | 31
    Solitude | 33
    Ordinary | 35

CONTENTS

CREEKS

Confidence | 41
Need | 43
Movement | 45
Spiritual | 47
Attention | 49
Friendship | 51
Newness | 53
Health | 55
Trails | 57
Remote | 59

RIVERS

Wild Places | 63
Discovery | 65
Nature | 67
Highpoints | 69
Faith | 71
Resistance | 73
Base Camp | 75
Alpine DNA | 77
Design | 79
Journey | 81

STREAMS

    Trust | 87
    Transformation | 89
    Resources | 90
    Truth | 91
    Reset | 93
    Breath | 95
    Reconciliation | 97
    Navigation | 99
    Discipline | 101
    Resilience | 103

5. To the Destination | 105

Endnotes | 107
Mountain Streams Playlist | 109

Forgetting your nature is death;
awareness is the condition for life.
ROWAN WILLIAMS

1.

From the Source

Restoring our nature has a double meaning: (1) living in the natural way, the way God designed us to live; and (2) preserving and protecting nature and wilderness by the way we live. The first meaning is the journey of faith and belief, while the second meaning explores earth science and stewardship. Both humans and nature belong to the created order.

Beginning with different premises, faith and science come out at the same conclusion. The Creator redeems/fulfills human nature and humans protect the natural world. Two mentors have guided me—one I knew well through my parents and by reading his 29 books; and one only from a distance. Both directed this dual journey which contains one purpose: restoring the created order.

Eli Stanley Jones was born in Baltimore and served in India for 66 years, reconciling individuals with the God who created them. Several relevant quotes of his are *my convictions* as well:

- *The Christian way is not an alien (strange or unknown) way; it is an affinity—the natural way to live. Here I come to perhaps the deepest conviction of my life, by my personal experience, and by the experience of all who have seriously tried it. I must surrender to the natural way.*

Mountain Streams

- *The conviction is this: I am made in my inner structure and outer relationships by Christ and for Christ; and when I find him, I find myself. And I find my brother (my humanity). I find how to live as an individual and as a member of society.*[1]

Aldo Leopold (1887–1948) was born in Burlington, Iowa, and lived in the same era as Stanley Jones, Leopold dying just before I was born. He was an American writer, philosopher, naturalist, scientist, ecologist, forester, conservationist, and environmentalist. He was assigned to the Forest Service's District 3 in the Arizona and New Mexico territories in 1909 and transferred to the Carson National Forest in northern New Mexico from 1911 to 1924. *I share his love for New Mexico and for wilderness preservation.*

He wrote the Forest Service's first game and fish handbook and proposed the preservation of the Gila Wilderness Area, the first national wilderness area, established in 1924. He served as a professor at the University of Wisconsin and is best known for his book *A Sand County Almanac* (1949). His ethics of nature and wildlife preservation had a profound impact on the environmental movement, with his eco-centric or holistic land ethic.

- *In wildness is the salvation of the world.*
- *The song of the waters is audible to every ear, but there is other music in these hills, by no means audible at all.*
- *On a still night, when the campfire is low and the Pleiades have climbed over rimrocks, sit quietly and listen, and think hard of everything you have seen and tried to understand.*[2]

Mountain streams have a literal and figurative meaning, symbolizing a path or a journey to a destination. The rivers, streams, creeks, and brooks literally carry life-giving water down to the villages, towns, and cities where the people live out their daily lives. The stream's movement and its music also quench our spiritual thirst, a gift from God, a promise of eternal life. *God wants to restore our nature, and we, in return, work to protect and preserve the natural world.*

From the Source

First, God. God is the subject of life. God is foundational for living. God created human nature to reflect divine nature. First, this: God created the Heavens and Earth—all you see, all you don't see. Earth was a soupy nothingness. God's Spirit brooded like a bird above the watery abyss.[3]

2.

The Eli Stanley Jones Stream

A Journey of Faith and Belief

Eli Stanley Jones was an American Christian missionary, teaching evangelist, and author whose first book, The Christ of the Indian Road, sold more than a million copies worldwide after its publication in 1925 and eventually three million copies by 2018. In 1938, Time Magazine called Jones the world's greatest missionary since St. Paul. He served in India from 1907 to 1973.

The reader can easily find extensive biographical information on Jones as well as his autobiography, A Song of Ascents. My desire in this account is to share a few personal lessons of faith and belief from my experience of his teachings, his writings, and my participation in the Christian Ashram movement which he founded in India (1930) and brought to the U.S. in 1940.

As he says in the introduction of his autobiography, "I owe much to the sons of men, but I owe everything to the Son of Man." Following the surrender of his life to Jesus Christ at age 17 under the preaching of Evangelist Robert Bateman and the prayers of his teacher Miss Nellie Logan, Jones attended Asbury College in Kentucky where he was called to missionary service in India. He was a young man of prayer and recounts that he told God that he would

The Eli Stanley Jones Stream

go wherever God sent him—accept a permanent teaching position at Asbury, serve in Africa, answer the call to India. One morning God replied, 'It's India.'"[4]

Human nature is redeemed and fulfilled by surrender to God. Jones repeatedly observed: "I cannot go down any road with any person on any issue without running right into the need for self-surrender." A phrase that we always used in college and campus ministry reiterates this truth: *Surrender all that you understand of yourself to all that you understand of God.*

Jones worked with the lowest castes in India including the Dalits and with many of the leaders in the Indian Independence movement, becoming well known for his Roundtable Conferences. He said, "Peace is a by-product of conditions out of which peace naturally comes. If reconciliation is God's chief business, it is ours too—between man and God, between man and himself, and between man and man." I would add "between mankind and nature." This is the created order.

Jones helped to re-establish the Indian "Ashram" (forest retreat) and founded the Christian Ashram movement as a means of drawing men and women together for weeks at a time to study their own spiritual natures and quest for meaning. "Ashram" is a Sanskrit word with a dual meaning: "away from work" and "to the work of the soul." The Christian Ashram was centered in Jesus Christ and in the historic confession "Jesus Is Lord!"

Jones was unapologetically a Christ-follower, initially at his moment of self-surrender and continually by daily surrender throughout his life. Theology is the study of God, and we are all theologians when we ask questions about the nature of God. Every quest begins with a question. Who am I? How do I become the person God created me to be? What is my life-purpose?

Jones did not develop a systematic theology or doctrinal system like so much Western Christianity today. He developed a Christology (Who do you say that I am? How do we follow Jesus in our cultural context?). His Christology determined his Missiology (how we go into all the world with God's Good News) and his

Ecclesiology (the fellowship and nature of the Church). Jones did not tend to use these big religious words.

Stanley Jones practiced the daily discipline of early morning prayer which he called "the listening post" and therefore he lived close to God. He found that God answers all prayers from the minute(small) to the magnificent(big). I recall one small story he recounted about losing and finding his eyeglasses at his beloved Sat Tal Ashram property in the foothills of the Himalayas.

One night walking up the mountainside he found that he had dropped his only pair of glasses. It was late and too dark to retrace his steps. All the time his inner voice in prayer kept saying, "You'll find your glasses." After several trips up and down the trail the next morning, he decided he must travel to the closest town to order new glasses which would take two weeks to arrive from Calcutta. As he was about to leave, he paused to tie his loose shoestring on a bridge railing and spotted his glasses down in the rocks. His gratitude was huge because without them he could not work on his book; but deeper he saw that miracles, big or little, like this one, were possible in a world of moral and physical law. He saw that "God works through the laws of nature" and "the law of redemptive purpose." God retrieves his own.

"I believe in miracle, but not too much miracle, for too much miracle would weaken us, make us dependent on miracle instead of our obedience to natural law." But this incident of the voice and the eyeglasses might have been a coincidence. It might have been. Another Stanley Jones story is about a big miracle.

Their daughter Eunice was attending the Woodstock School in India and was diagnosed as having tuberculosis. Jones was at the hill station at Sat Tal when his wife wired him that they must take Eunice to Switzerland for treatment. Sitting outside under a tree at morning devotions, concerned about his daughter's illness Jones heard the inner voice quietly but convincingly say, "She will be well." He couldn't substitute his inner voice for the doctor's verdict. As he was preparing to leave Sat Tal, he knew inwardly that they would never go, that she would be well. The doctor at the school examined her again and found only some scar tissue but nothing active. They didn't need to make the trip and Eunice was well and has been the rest of her life.

I knew Eunice for the last 25 years of her life until her death at age 101. God does heal through big miracles! Stanley Jones said daily, "I'm fresh in the Lord." *He lived close to God.*

3 ·

The Aldo Leopold Stream

Exploring the Earth and Its Stewardship

Aldo Leopold was an American writer, naturalist, forester, conservationist, and scientist and is best known for his book *A Sand County Almanac* (1949) which has sold more than two million copies. In 1900, Gifford Pinchot, who oversaw the newly implemented Division of Forestry in the Department of Agriculture, donated money to Yale University to begin one of the nation's first forestry schools. Hearing of this development, the teenaged Leopold decided on forestry as a vocation.

Leopold's early life was highlighted by the outdoors because his father would take his children on excursions into the woods and teach his son woodcraft and hunting. Aldo showed an aptitude for observation, spending hours counting and cataloging birds near his home. He was very much an outdoorsman, even in his extreme youth. He was always out climbing around the bluffs, or going down to the river, or going across the river into the woods.

After graduating from the Yale Forestry School in 1909, he was assigned to the Forest Service's District 3 in the Arizona and New Mexico territories. Leopold's career kept him in New Mexico until 1924 and included developing the first comprehensive management plan for the Grand Canyon, writing the Forest Service's first game and fish handbook, and proposing Gila Wilderness Area as the nation's first national wilderness area.

In 1933, as a Professor of Game Management and Research Director at the University of Wisconsin, Leopold and other members of the Arboretum Committee re-established "Original Wisconsin" landscape and plant communities. These communities of tallgrass prairie and oak savanna predated European settlement. Leopold's nature writing is notable for its simple directness. His portrayals of natural environments display impressive intimacy with what exists and happens in nature.

It is warm behind the driftwood now, for the wind has gone with the geese. So would I—if I were the wind. (A Sand County Almanac)[5]

"Aldo Leopold was not merely the 'father' of the conservation movement, or restoration, or so many other fields of knowledge that derive from his philosophy, fieldwork, and scholarly work. His ideas remain ahead of our times despite his eloquence that so moves his readers. Maybe the world will finally discover him and implement his seminal contribution, a land ethic."
–Richard Nisbett,
Sanctuary Scientist and Publicist.[6]

On the Land:

- We abuse land because we regard it as a commodity belonging to us. When we see land as a community to which we belong, we may begin to use it with love and respect.—Aldo Leopold[7]

- Land is not merely soil, it is a fountain of energy flowing through a circuit of soils, plants, and animals.
- Conservation is a state of harmony between man and land.
- There can be no doubt that a society rooted in the soil is more stable than one rooted in pavements.

On the Wilderness:

- If we lose our wilderness, we have nothing left worth fighting for.
- A river or a stream is a cycle of energy from sun to plants to insects to fish. It is a continuum broken only by humans.
- There are some who can live without wild things, some who cannot. For us of the minority, the opportunity to see geese is more important than television.

Leopold was influential in the development of modern environmental ethics and in the movement for wilderness preservation. His ethics of nature and wildlife conservation had a profound impact on the environmental movement and holistic ethics regarding land. He emphasized biodiversity and ecology and was a founder of the science of wildlife management.

Early in his career, Leopold was assigned to hunt and kill bears, wolves, and mountain lions in New Mexico. Local ranchers hated these predators because of livestock losses, but Leopold came to respect the animals. One day after fatally shooting a wolf, Aldo reached the animal and was transfixed by a "fierce green fire dying in her eyes."[8] That experience changed him and put him on the path toward an eco-centric outlook.

He developed an ecological ethic that replaced the earlier wilderness ethic that had stressed the need for human dominance. His rethinking the importance of predators in the balance of nature has resulted in the return of bears and mountain lions to New

The Aldo Leopold Stream

Mexico wilderness areas. Leopold believed that it is easier to maintain the wilderness than to create it.

In 1935, he helped found the Wilderness Society, dedicated to expanding and protecting the nation's wilderness areas. He regarded the Society as "one of the focal points of a new attitude—an intelligent humility toward Man's place in nature. The concept of a trophic cascade is put forth in the chapter, "Thinking Like a Mountain," from A Sand County Almanac, wherein Leopold realizes that killing a predatory wolf carries serious implications for the rest of the ecosystem.

The Aldo Leopold Neighborhood Historic District in Albuquerque, New Mexico, comprises a single block on the west side of 14th Street south of Central Avenue, as the residence of noted naturalist Aldo Leopold. It was added to the National Register of Historic Places in 2002. *Leopold preferred the wilderness.*

4.

Reflections

Brooks, Creeks, Rivers, and Streams are categories for my Reflections from basic spiritual principles to advanced practices of faith. A brook, a creek, a river, and a stream begin in the mountains and high places and flow down to us from somewhere above. God is the architect of creation—both visible and invisible. The visible creation includes plants, animals, humankind, wildlife, sea life, the sun, moon, stars, and planets, mountains, valleys, forests, rivers, lakes, and oceans are God's handiwork.

Exploration in the mountains and wilderness areas enhances the visible natural realm. The invisible creation includes everything in the spiritual realm. Enter that realm cautiously when you walk, praying and contemplating. The visible and the invisible, humans and nature comprise the created order.

My Reflections connect the formative realities of redeemed human nature with the restored natural world. God formed the entire created order and re-forms humans, positively changing those who choose to live close to God. We live fully alive by relationships not by religious rules and redemption requires a divine intervention. Modern religion has become mesmerized by the appeal of escape from this world rather than redemption for this world, permitting man's relentless assault on God's creation.

Reflections

Redeemed people are made for movement, flowing like a mountain stream. We are moving toward the future. We move in faith. We move toward people, even when we must go to our extraverted side. We move toward God. We are moving toward eternity. We are not meant to sit, soak, and sour. We are made to move. We are forward-looking people, flowing through wild places to our destination, a renewed heaven and earth.

BROOKS

*natural but small rivulets
of running water*

Restoration

Restoration in sacred writings is synonymous with healing, repairing, recovering the joy and strength of the Creator. The Psalmist wrote about the restoration of the joy of wholeness and the joy of a willing spirit. God is the Holy Mountain, the Source of Life. God is the Fountain of Living Waters.

When I was a child and my parents said, "we're going to the mountains," I was always excited. The trip was usually a brief foray into the Sangre de Cristo mountains of northern New Mexico and southern Colorado only three to four hours from our home in a small Texas Panhandle town. Up in Cimarron Canyon where the Cimarron River flows down from Eagle Nest Lake there was a small general store and log cabin with a drinking log protruding from a fresh stream. We would always make a stop there to drink the pure mountain water flowing out of that log.

We would fill our canteens and water bottles for our weekend camping adventure and select a campsite close by one of the rivers or streams in this forested, narrow canyon. We fished and often caught trout. The earthy scent of pine and juniper and the rich forest floor made my spirit willing to explore. I learned to be at home in the wilderness there and accept its soul refreshment.

The mountains have always provided restoration for the soul and an eternal perspective. There is a certainty in the rocks and spires and peaks that contrast sharply with the flighty and frivolous human constructs. They call us to something higher and deeper and cause us to look up to the mountains. *God made the mountains.* Sing this song of ascent on your personal pilgrimage.

God creates and God restores. "Morning has broken like the first morning, God's re-creation of the new day."[9] Participate in creation. Leave the city of man. Seek the living waters, high in the mountains. The mountains remind us that the firm foundation supporting us is God's goodness, joy, and strength, flowing to restore us.

Receptivity

The First Law of the Spiritual Life is the Law of Receptivity—you can only give out what you have taken in; release what you've received. Any living organism, from a flower to a human being, must receive, *before* they can give. It may be "more blessed to give than to receive" but receiving precedes giving. No water comes from a dry spring.

Often when I am hiking in the mountains, I can feel the coolness from the heights and hear the underground streams trickle down before I see the refreshing streams of water. Higher up, the snow is melting, or an alpine lake is overflowing. There are hidden springs that I hear before I see the creeks and rivers. "I am about to do something new. I will make a pathway through the wilderness and streams of water in the dry and empty land." (Psalm 43:19 NASB)

On my 2023 climb of Blanca Peak in Colorado, I was thoroughly soaked by an unexpected rainstorm just before midnight. Travelling in my ultralight way I had no tent nor change of clothes. As I searched at the 13,000-foot level in the dark for some minimal shelter, I stumbled across hidden streams covered by vegetation. Blanca Peak is one of the four sacred peaks of the Navajo people, and it did occur to me that the gods were unhappy with my alpine intrusion. The true God said I will make a pathway through the wilderness.

Looking up I saw several merging ridges and realized my nocturnal wanderings were ending in a box canyon. The pathway through the high-country wilderness became obvious. I needed to descend toward the trees below. The streams led me down. The mountains can be some of life's greatest teachers. Listen to their language, to the babbling brook and the whistling wind.

The mountains remind us that God lights the paths we walk, gives us direction, and reveals a way where there is no way.

Mystery

In the Psalms, mountains are viewed as sacred and central to the experiences of the holy land. Several passages proclaim their goodness and beauty: "Mount Zion! The perfection of beauty! Breathtaking in its heights!" (Psalm 48:2 NASB). Mountainous heights inspire vision and the virtues that flow from them like peace and righteousness.

The sacred mountains of the Southwest protect the sacred homeland of the Diné, the People, as the Navajo call themselves. The four sacred mountains of the Navajo extend from the San Francisco Peaks of Arizona in the west to the Sangre de Cristo Range of Colorado and New Mexico to the east. These four are Humphries Peak in Arizona, Blanca Peak in Colorado, Mount Taylor in New Mexico, and Mount Hesperus in Colorado.

The native people mark their territory by, but do not typically climb, these mountains. As one Hopi man told author Edwin Bernbaum, "we go to the mountains to pray quietly." The mountains provide the sense of order needed to restore the spiritual harmony and balance that a person requires for physical health and well-being. I went to each of the four mountains to climb them and I have a cautionary story from each one.

My abbreviated version is this: lightning chased us off Humphries; nighttime rainstorms soaked me on Blanca; a wrong turn isolated and delayed me on Taylor. I desperately wanted to climb the fourth sacred peak—Hesperus—in September 2023. We drove to Colorado from Albuquerque hoping to easily ascend Hesperus (13,238 feet) as a warm-up before climbing several 14ers in the San Juans. Hesperus turned into a tough climb.

Mountain deities aside, I can explain our challenges with science: predictable summer thunderstorms; erroneous weather forecast; and poor trail signage and maintenance. The spiritual truth falls closer to this: *the sacred is a mystery best unexplained but lived.*

Eternity

Infinity and eternity are not the same thing. *Infinity* is a numerical term meaning "indefinitely large" or "endless." *Eternity* is not "time without end." *Eternity* is the end of time. Climbing to the summit of a Colorado 14er just last year, I had an experience of eternity that happens sometimes on high mountain summits.

As I gazed at mountains 360 degrees in all directions, time seemed suspended. In some ways the gray rock and snow-covered peaks surrounding me all looked the same. We experience "time" in different ways. When time seems to slow down or stop, we say things like "time stood still" or "I was unaware of time passing." You've no doubt known this feeling.

Sometimes hours seem like minutes, usually when we are doing what we were created to do and love doing. And sometimes minutes seem like hours. Time doesn't stop but appears to really slow down. *The days are long, but the years fly by.*

In the silence of the mountains, time markers do seem less relevant. Peter Matthiessen, author of *The Snow Leopard*, writes: "Snow mountains, more than sea or sky, serve as a mirror to one's own true being, utterly still, utterly clear, a void, an Emptiness without life or sound that carries in itself all life, all sound."[10] *Eternity contains within it all time.*

Here and now, we measure time. We measure seconds, minutes, hours, days, weeks, months, years, decades, and centuries. Eternity is not measurable. Eternal life is real, but it does not just go on and on and on . . . Eternity is the end of time because it is outside of time. We often say, "eternity means everlasting." I think eternal really means God-life, life with God. "With the

Lord one day is as a thousand years, and a thousand years as one day." (2 Peter 3:8 NASB). *Stand on a tall mountain, gaze at a mystery not yet seen.*

Early

Mountain climbers rise early, while it is still dark. In many mountain ranges like the Rockies, it is best to summit before noon, ahead of the thunderstorms that often build at midday. Lightning is the number one cause of death in the high country. On snow and ice mountains, the footing is better before the morning sun and warmer temps begin to melt frozen surfaces.

Many summit day climbs begin as early as midnight so that the team can reach the top by sunrise. On Kilimanjaro in 2007, we reached Uhuru Peak (19,341 feet) just as the sun was rising. It was a clear day—what I call a bluebird day--on the roof of Africa. As I looked North that morning, I could see Mount Kenya 320 kilometers or 200 miles away. In 2009, I summited Mt. Kenya on another bluebird day and saw Kilimanjaro 320 km to the South!

In June 2007, our team awoke early at Camp Muir for our 2:00 a.m. start to Mt. Rainier's summit. We enjoyed clear night skies over the Cowlitz Glacier and the sunrise came as we traversed the Ingraham Glacier to the base of Disappointment Cleaver. Then the weather began to change. Clouds descended on the upper third of the mountain. The formation of this cloudcap created hazardous visibility conditions. A team member below us fell into a crevasse and was rescued, delaying our progress. Making the summit that morning, there was no view.

I still love an early start to my day and rising long before dawn. Despite the risks from climbing in the dark, it has become my alpine routine. When I see a line of headlamps moving up the mountain while it is still night, I am inspired to get going myself.

I am also reminded of the great number of early risers, mountain climbers, and prayer warriors who have gone before me.

There is a saying: *Early to bed, early to rise, makes a man healthy, wealthy, and wise.* Well, I would at least say *healthy.*

Refill

I have camped beside waterfalls in the wilderness above 13,000 feet, some a simple cascade falling in stages down a rocky slope and some a vertical spectacle in freefall. We need the water for drinking and cooking, and their constant cascading sound creates nights of good rest. *But you can't stay at the waterfall.* You can fill your water bottles and carry bags for the climb. The water leaves the waterfall and flows down the mountain and refills lakes and reservoirs below. God refills our spiritual reservoirs.

At the end of the Sermon on the Mountain, Jesus reminds us that the one who is wise builds his or her life on solid principles. Let God refill your reservoir. The streams rise and the winds blow, be wise and not foolish. Your reservoir needs refilling. God's living water is descending and flowing to fill your *inner* well.

High in the backcountry wilderness of the Sangre de Cristo Mountains in Colorado, I was hiking alone in the night, going on the wrong trail. My mental thoughts considered this but then I heard in my spirit, "Now it's time to change directions." Turn to face God so that times of refreshing may come from God's presence. "Repent" literally means "turn around." Make a 180 degree turn and go in the opposite direction. Let God renew and refresh you. Exchange your routine for rhythms of nature.

G.K. Chesterton wrote, "An adventure is, by its nature, a thing that comes to us. It is a thing that chooses us, not a thing we choose."[11] *It is not an adventure until something goes wrong.*[12] I believe adventures choose us, become a way of exploring ourselves as much as exploring mountains or any wilderness. We discover the need to move and the need to rest.

I will show you how to take a real rest. Learn the unforced rhythms of unmerited favor. Let God refill you.

Rhythm

"And of Joseph he said . . . Blessed by the LORD be his land, with the choicest gifts of heaven above . . . with the best things of the ancient mountains and with the choice things of the everlasting hills." (Deuteronomy 33:13 NASB). This is one of the blessings with which Moses, God's man, blessed the people of Israel before his own death and eternal rest.

What are the "best and choice things" of the mountains and the hills? Hills and mountains provide water from snowmelt and underground springs for drinking and growing food. Water is life! The best things may also be the trees . . . the cedars and the hardwoods for construction . . . the fruit and olive trees for food.

Many mountainous and forested regions of the world provide timber for our homes and lodges. Productive hillsides produce an abundance of crops and orchards for our sustenance. These "choice things" include what is ancient, an everlasting rhythm.

My treks into and over the mountains have also produced these choice things: perspiration, inspiration, and aspiration. Hard work, hope, and heightened adventure. If we go to the beach to observe the ocean tides, we go into the mountains to climb up for a sweeping view, a vision of where we are going.

I woke up in my backpacking tent at 3:00 o'clock in the Wind River Range of Wyoming on an August morning. We had just summited the state's highest mountain, Gannett Peak, on day five of an eight-day climbing trek. I had been climbing 8–10 peaks a year and my son Shawn joined me when he could. We climbed Kilimanjaro together as well as many Colorado 14ers.

Laying in my sleeping bag resisting the desire to venture outside, the "Three Secrets" burst into my mind in the thin Wyoming air:

Tell me where you're going. Tell me who is going with you. Tell me what resources you will need. Climb for a bigger vision!

Exploring

Observe the way he climbs mountains and the way he lives his life. (A reference to Yvon Chouinard, climber and founder of the Patagonia company.) I like another saying about Chouinard, 'he's never been a peak bagger. The route on a mountain has always been the only thing that mattered to him. The quality of the route, not the summit.' Consider your route through wild places.

I am learning to climb like that and to teach my grandchildren to find the cleanest line on the boulders behind our cabin at the lake. I hope one part of my legacy will be a love of the outdoors and wilderness preservation. I recommend the book by author Richard Louv entitled *Last Child in the Woods—Saving Our Children from Nature-Deficit Disorder.*

My wife and I were in Anchorage for an economic development conference and explored museums, art galleries, and great eating establishments. We made several side trips to Seward on the Alaska Railway Train and the Kenai Fjords by a day-long boat trip. I was eager to get into the Chugach Mountains and to drive north to Talkeetna for a view of Denali. As Bilbo Baggins said many times, 'I want to see mountains again, mountains Gandalf!'

I rented a car and drove to the Glen Arms TH for a snow climb of Flattop Mountain. The lower trail was slushy and wet while the upper section was covered with 10–12 inches of snow. The crux was a steep trough with 18–20 inches of new snow and spindrift blowing constantly in my face. I climbed slowly, finding handholds buried in the snow and kicking steps for solid toe holds. I descended from the summit backing down my same route. It was good to climb today and enjoy a light supper with Lou Ann back in Anchorage. Never Stop Exploring!

We are dependent on the existence of wild places in the world, even when we rarely visit the wilderness. We know it exists.

Solitude

Mountains tend to be solitary places, as difficult as they are beautiful. It takes time, and skill and care to climb them, a kind of humility. Mountains lend perspective—the noisy life of the valley fades and suddenly all the achievements of human civilization, our tall skyscrapers, our bustling cities, become quiet against the peaks. (Sutterfield)[13]

Most climbs are better shared, preferably with a trusted and skilled climbing partner. Despite knowing this truth personally, I've done my share of solo climbs: Mt. Shasta, Granite Peak, Mt. Harvard, Mt. Elbert, Mt. Massive, Mt. Shavano, Blanca Peak, Mt. Princeton, Mt. Yale, Mt. Columbia, Mt. Kenya, Humphries Peak, among others. My solo climbs have been motivated by a desire for solitude, alone in nature.

Mountain summits—like any mountaintop experience—bring clarity and perspective. We see things more clearly, set apart beyond time and place. In our overcrowded urban environments, we are seldom alone for long. My wilderness perspective? You don't have to take an extended backpacking trip in Colorado for some solitude. God wants "alone time" with you. It matters.

"True solitude is found in the wild places, where one is without human obligation. The more coherent one becomes with oneself as a creature, the more fully one enters into the communion of all creatures."[14] (Wendell Berry) In God, all things are coherent, hold together, make sense.

Many of my solo climbs have been in Colorado and I would like to share another dimension of my Harvard climb with the reader. After climbing Mt. Yale and Mt. Princeton in the Collegiate Peaks Range, thunderstorms filled the high country with heavy rain and snow showers at higher elevations. Planning to climb Mt. Harvard next, I had to hit "pause" and rent a cabin at Vista Court in Buena Vista. God engineers our circumstances and sometimes changes our plans. *God directs our steps.*

My weather delay caused these observations: I am spending a lot of time in nature and my God-given vocation is enriched by time in the natural world. Life makes more sense.

Ordinary

> Eric Shipton and Bill Tilman—worldwide icons to all those interested in mountain adventure—climbed during the 1930s, the great decade of British Himalayan exploration. Shipton and Tilman did not go to the mountains to be considered extraordinary. They went out of simple curiosity, and they moved through them in the least intrusive manner possible, with indigenous people they regarded and treated not as underlings, but as friends. Their ordinary selves have become our best examples. (Perrin)

When I began to do serious backpacking trips into remote wilderness areas, I carried heavy packs with extra clothing and gear that I never used. I was young and strong. Three-week trips in the Teton and Yellowstone Wilderness areas did require preparation for all kinds of weather and terrain. "Be prepared" was the Scout motto and I tended to overprepare.

Leave No Trace. I learned to "move through (the mountains) less intrusively." *Travel light* became my motto as ultralight gear was developed. I learned the layering system, clothed simply for life in the mountains. My son Shawn was a well-dressed naval officer, but in our wilderness adventures it was he who taught me simplicity, wearing his tattered jeans and old wool sweater there. We are at home in the mountains.

20th Century Christian mystic Thomas Merton wrote in *The Wisdom of the Desert*, "simple men who lived their lives out to a good old age among the rocks and sand only did so because they had come into the desert to be themselves, their *ordinary* selves, and to forget a world that divided them from themselves."[15] *Mountains help me remain human and ordinary.*

CREEKS

*a small stream of water
often a tributary to a river*

Confidence

The wonderfully clear days, the sight of a new rock beyond the snow rise, the tremendous feeling of freedom among the mountains and glaciers, the close comradeship which develops in isolated groups from shared experience and the growth of mutual confidence: these are lasting memories.
(Fuchs)[16]

Memory and memories, short-term and long-term, are personal, individual recollections. *Memory* is the faculty by which the mind stores and remembers information. *Memories* are something remembered from the past. Memory is a continually unfolding process. Memories reflect real-world experience, but with varying levels of fidelity to that original experience.

I have encoded into my memory more alpine experiences with my son and climbing partner Shawn not only because of personal significance but also because of mutual confidence. I am confident in his skills and judgement. He trusts my climbing skills and judgement. He is a trustworthy person.

We've climbed many mountains together, none more isolated than peaks in the San Juan Mountains, Colorado's finest range. The San Juan reality for these 13 fourteeners is rotten rock and jagged wilderness. The wild, rugged peaks of the Eolus Group are the most remote of Colorado's 14ers. Eolus, Sunlight, and Windom guard the zenith of Colorado fourteener experience. Shawn and I climbed them in 2018.

Climbing builds mutual confidence, resulting in a clearer trust in things beyond memory.

Need

If these mountains die, where will our imaginations wander? If the far mesas are leveled, what will sustain us in our quest to be larger than life? If the high valley is made mundane by self-seekers and careless users, where we will find another landscape so eager to nourish our love? And if the longtime people of this wonderful country are carelessly squandered by Progress, who will guide us to a better world? (Nichols)[17]

While our natural resources and mountainous wilderness areas are certainly under siege today, the John Nichols quote above serves as a reminder of a deep human need. Remote mountain ranges and their geographical importance fill a God-given desire planted within each person. We need a sense of place, a sense of provision, and a sense of purpose. Mountains and mesas, high valleys and vistas, alpine lakes and landscapes locate us by a spiritual GPS. We have a primitive human desire to be situated in a refuge with a view.

Two climbs that we made in 2021, Uncompahgre and Wetterhorn, are situated as the most northern peaks in the San Juan

Mountains and the view from their summits includes fourteeners in every direction. Uncompahgre is Colorado's sixth highest peak and the Native American word from the Ute Nation meaning "hot-water spring." Colorado's Wetterhorn is named after the extant Wetterhorn rising above Grindelwald in Switzerland's Bernese Alps. Wetterhorn means "weather peak" in German. These are two of my favorite Colorado fourteeners with their sweeping panorama!

Mountaineers seek the uncharted way, the trail less traveled, and a summit to stand on. The wilderness we seek is a resource that we must protect, an innate human need.

Movement

Galen Rowell was a man who went into the mountains, into the desert, to the edge of the sea, to the last great wild places in the world to be absorbed by their grace and grandeur. That is what he did for himself. For the rest of us, he shared his vision with—click—the release of a shutter, creating photographs as timeless, as stunning, and as powerful as nature itself. (Tom Brokaw)[18]

In the late 1970s we spent three weeks hiking and camping in the backcountry of Yellowstone National Park, studying local geology there. I especially remember the striations on the boulders marking the retreat of gigantic glaciers. Twice I have backpacked and climbed in Yosemite National Park. These two National Parks exhibit the *grace and grandeur* that inspires those who explore them, beyond the paved roads.

We need grace and grandeur. Grace can be defined as simple elegance and refinement of movement as well as goodwill and good manners. Grandeur can refer to high rank and social importance, but in the natural world it means splendor and impressive, as in "the grandeur of mountain scenery." Perhaps what seems lost in human nature today can be restored by learning from the splendor and elegance found in nature. Mountaineering and outdoor photography embody movement and that which is always moving.

Movement in mountain climbing progresses through levels and stages of growing toward goals. I've observed this natural process in gaining alpine skills: acclimate to altitude -> explore the easy -> move into moderate -> expand your exposure -> venture into vertical -> tackle the technical. Result? *Grace and grandeur inspired by the landscape.*

Spiritual

> *From the Andes to the Himalayas, mountains have an extraordinary power to evoke a sense of the sacred. In the overwhelming wonder and awe that these dramatic features of the landscape awaken, people experience something of deeper significance that imbues their lives with meaning and vitality. Sacred mountains have enriched my life, elevated my gaze, and broadened my horizons in ways I could never have imagined. (Bernbaum)*[19]

We humans have a natural desire in our lives for meaning and purpose. Some who search today are searching desperately for significance. Some look within themselves and many pursue external events and happenings. Happiness is elusive. If your search drives you to the mountains, go! We don't worship the mountains. Just because you love the mountains doesn't mean the mountains love you.

The idea that mountains are sacred refers to the fact that people connect them with God (or the gods) and for that reason the mountain is venerated or revered. Mountains all over the world are considered sacred and the people of their respective region worship or pray to those mountains. For me, mountains, deserts, and remote unpopulated places are more spiritual than sacred. These are inhospitable to human habitation. We enter these places as seekers and guests.

My Dad and I climbed New Mexico's highest mountain, Wheeler Peak, several times together. I've climbed it alone in winter, climbed it with my daughter carrying her two-year-old son, and climbed it with my brother Rick to scatter dad's ashes from the summit. Rick remained at Williams Lake where the elevation (11,000 feet) was affecting his breathing.

Alone on the very top that day, I went to the edge, to a thin place, to a far horizon. The wind stream quickly took dad's ashes out of sight. Imagine the spiritual kingdom.

Attention

Mountains are a dominant feature of the religious landscape and have influenced greatly the way of life and beliefs of people, ancient and modern. Mountains have important effects upon the climate, population, economic life, and state of civilization of the region in which they occur. Lands on their windward side have greater rainfall, while those on the leeward side are arid.

One of the best lessons you learn in the mountains is that they create their own weather. Forecasts and weather apps are important to climbers in the backcountry, but it can often seem like the mountain has a mind of its own. Every year climbers die on Mount Hood in the Cascades when invisible or unexpected forces like whiteout blizzards or rapidly moving weather systems slam them. Mount Hood creates its own weather.

Two climbing partners and I were blinded by a blizzard at the top of the Palmer Glacier in June 2007. Most climbing injuries and deaths on Mt. Hood occur when inexperienced or ill-equipped climbers are hit by falling rock, ice, or snow; they slip down steep slopes or into crevasses; or they become disoriented in poor weather conditions. *Pay attention to the weather and to climate. They are not the same.*

Mountains have effects on climate and climate has effects on mountains. These are five benefits that mountains provide: (1) a home for almost 1.1 billion people; (2) about half of all the world's biodiversity hotspots; (3) the origin of 6 out the 20 most important food crops; (4) forests that cover around 40% of the global mountain area; and (5) up to 60—80% of the world's fresh water.[20]

Water, soil, nitrogen, oxygen, forests, trees, plants, bees, birds, seeds, thrive in the wild, uninhabited places.

Whatever your belief system or worldview, mountains are essential to human life. They send water downstream. Pay attention to the natural world and find your place in it.

Friendship

Mountaineering is many things. It is climbing, panoramic views, and wilderness experience. For many, it is the fulfillment of childhood dreams; for others, an opportunity to grow in the face of difficulty. In the mountains await adventure and mystery and lifetime bonds with climbing partners. The challenge of mountaineering offers you a chance to learn about yourself outside the confines of the modern world. (The Freedom of the Hills)

Kent Barnard and I had lunch together in January 2024 at his home in Waco, Texas, spending most of our time recalling the mountains we had climbed together. Originally from Bakersfield, California, where he lived most of his life, Kent and I first met at the Redwood Christian Park north of Santa Cruz in July 2000. It was an instant friendship.

Kent discovered that I was hiking and climbing the state highpoints and indicated an interest to join me when I was ready to tackle the big mountains of the Western U.S. That conversation sparked a climbing partnership which became a deep friendship.

Without Kent's Toyota Prius, my 50 Peaks Challenge would not have happened.

We did some climbing in California, made my first trip to Yosemite for some hiking, and began to plan our western states highpoints. We climbed Boundary Peak in Nevada and Mt. Whitney in California in July 2006. Then we did Kings Peak in Utah and Borah Peak in Idaho in September 2006. The next summer we climbed Mt. Rainier in Washington and Mt. Hood in Oregon. In 2008 we climbed Gannett Peak in Wyoming.

Whoever walks with people of wisdom becomes wise.

Newness

Author Jim Perrin distinguishes mountain travel from mountaineering in his biography of British climbers Eric Shipton and Bill Tilman. Writer Mark Cocker highlights the psychology of travel highly relevant to Shipton's mountain travel and climbing: "Few experiences are better able to reveal the unconscious mind to the conscious than travel."[21] Perrin continues by making the following statement:

"Having stressed the way in which the literature of travel often dramatizes a return to the innocence and paradise of childhood, Perrin outlines the psychological effect: By loosening the mental restraints that secure our adult relationship to the world, travel often initiates a state of consciousness that is extremely similar to childhood. In journeys we discover again the newness of the world."[22]

Many people love to be in the mountains without climbing difficult summits and rock spires. Backcountry hikers and expedition walkers experience the world in new ways. In the summer of 1977, Lou Ann and I spent three weeks hiking and backpacking in Wyoming, camping for nine days in the wilderness west of the Tetons. The word "expedition" means "to leave on foot."

The Tetons expedition did take me back to my childhood hikes, exploring the creeks and caves of Rita Blanca Canyon. Around the age of 10, I joined my dad and some Scout leaders on a week-long hike in Northern New Mexico and the Philmont Scout ranch. Beyond childhood memories, the Tetons trip contained so many seed moments for my future.

It triggered my lifelong commitment to running, to mountain travel, to exploration, and to seeing daily the newness of life. And it did something else. I became at home in the mountain wilderness. God set me secure on the heights. He gave me energy, swiftness, and, above all, sure-footedness. Nerve was defined by a small boy as "walking along awfully high walls and liking it." That is what the mountain goat does.

I know. I've seen them. Goats are confident on the rocks and secure on the high places. In the things of the mind and conscience, where others hesitate and are afraid, the person who is constantly God-referred walks with steady steps. And it is more. God wants us "on the heights" while promising His presence there with us.

"To Him who is able to keep you from falling and to present you before His glorious presence without fault and with great joy." (Jude 24–25 NASB).

Health

While high altitude mountaineering, mountain and big wall climbing, and backcountry skiing claim lives every season, there are certain health benefits the mountains provide. Living and spending time at altitude is correlated with rates of higher longevity, lower obesity, and better physical and mental health. The mountain environment is associated with our spiritual health as well. Walk among the sacred peaks.

My dad lived most of his life at an elevation of 4000 feet, ran and walked daily, and frequently travelled and hiked in the mountains of Northern New Mexico. There are other reasons and factors that contribute to his health and long life. He loved people and he was a man who prayed with and for people. Studies of prayer have been associated with better health and longer life. Dad lived 96 years and 8 days.

Consider these alpine benefits to physical health: stronger hearts and lungs, better balance and coordination, and increased leg and arm strength. Mountains have positive effects on your state of mind: reduced stress and anxiety, increased endorphins to boost mood, and better sleep. You can connect with your spiritual side in the mountains: find a renewed sense of purpose, discover an inner peace through solitude and reflection, and be more present in nature.

The mountains and hills will burst into song before you. All the trees in the forest will be exuberant with applause. The stately and scented pines will be a living and lasting evidence of God who formed the mountains by his power.

May the mountains bring peace and prosperity to the people, healing the body, mind, and soul.

Trails

The National Trails System is a series of trails in the United States designated to promote the preservation, public access to, travel within, and enjoyment of the open-air, outdoor areas and historic resources of the Nation. The scenic and historic trails are in every state, and Virginia and Wyoming have the most trails running through them, with six. Historically, many trails were wildlife and big game trails as well as well-worn pathways of Native peoples.

I have hiked sections of the Appalachian Trail and the Pacific Crest Trail which are National Scenic Trails as well as walked the wagon ruts of the Santa Fe Trail and portions of the Nez Perce Trail which are National Historic Trails. The System in the U.S. consists of 11 national scenic trails, 21 national historic trails, over 1300 national recreation trails, and seven connecting and side trails, with one national geologic trail. This constitutes more than 91,000 miles of trails.

Growing up I walked trails in the Texas Panhandle where the Apache, Comanche, and Kiowa peoples had travelled, places like Palo Duro Canyon and the playa lakes of the Llano Estacado prairies. I hunted and collected arrowheads, spear points, and scrapers from ancient campgrounds and flint quarries. My dominant memory of these places and hikes is the wind which always sweeps across the plains, the vast horse country. Memory is a strong spirit.

When I enter a wilderness area or a national forest at a designated trailhead, I think of the people who have blazed these trails before me. In New Mexico and Colorado, I know that Native peoples preceded my explorations by centuries. I also know that the land sustained them but belonged to no one person or group.

Wilderness areas are wild places that evoke mystery and wonder, where the earth and its community of life are untrammeled by man, where man himself is a visitor who does not remain. These places are wild landscapes that present nature in its rawest form.

"Ask for the ancient paths, the good way, and walk the trails as you pass through life." (Jeremiah 6:16 NASB).

Remote

On my six-foot long pine work desk, sits a photography book titled *Let's Get Lost: The World's Most Stunning Remote Locations*. It is filled with spectacular photographs from 30 remote places in the world, divided into six sections: mountains, wilderness, coast, ice & snow, lakes & rivers, and forests. Why do photographs of far-off places capture our imagination so vividly?

From the book's introduction by Finn Beales comes his answer: "Perhaps we are simply seeking an escape from the rigors of everyday life, but I think it's more than that. Our curiosity to explore runs deep; it's hardwired. Exploring improves our understanding of new places and can also lead to a more profound perception of ourselves."[23]

While I have been in some very remote places, only three of 30 remote places in *Let's Get Lost* were places I had visited. Volcanoes National Park, Hawaii, USA; White Sands, New Mexico, USA; and Antarctica; the first two are in the Wilderness section and the third one is in the Ice & Snow section. My photographs from these journeys (as well as others) do not begin to compare to the professional photos. Still, even the pictures taken in my mind are indelibly imprinted like a watermark in my character.

Speaking about another outdoor photographer, Galen Rowell, Tom Brokaw wrote: "He understood that nature in all its glory and heart-stopping capacity truly is an intricate tribute to the many forces, seen and unseen, that shape the world around us. His legs were as important as his eye in taking us to these remote and wild places."[24] Let's get lost and see what we find!

RIVERS

*a large stream of water
with considerable volume*

Wild Places

Rick Ridgeway is a mountaineering legend who is known for his writing, photography, and filmmaking. He has led a celebrated life of adventure, reflected on what drives true explorers, and provided poignant insights into how we relate to wild places. "If you really want to climb more mountains, that's what you'll do. The wanting to is the hard part."[25]

Wild places for most outdoor enthusiasts mean mountains, national forests, and designated wilderness areas. Wilderness and wildlands are natural environments on Earth that have not been significantly modified by human activity. The term has traditionally referred to land-based environments, though growing attention is placed on marine wilderness.

Recent maps of wilderness suggest it covers roughly one-quarter of Earth's terrestrial surface, but is being rapidly degraded by human activity, such as destruction of Amazon rainforests. In my writing I encourage people to spend time exploring the wilderness as a means of personal and spiritual growth. People are doing that. But more people impact wilderness adversely. Protecting and preserving wild places for future generations becomes harder.

Never Stop Exploring and Get Outdoors are corporate slogans that promote outdoor clothing and gear but may inadvertently contribute to the overuse of public lands. *My grandfather spoke of a time before fences, of endless forests and trees. We've got to have wilderness, if we want to be free.*

Granddad Valentine had Irish blood running through his veins, earning his livelihood from ranching and dryland farming in New Mexico and Oldham County in the Texas Panhandle.

He raised cattle in scrub oak and juniper hills east of the Sandia Mountains, making long cattle drives to markets in Kansas City and St. Louis. Farming in the Panhandle was a hard life but a life of hard work and open country, wild and free.

Later in life Granddad had a rural mail route that he drove every morning. I loved riding with him on those dusty unpaved roads to deliver letters and packages. And Granddad Valentine took me to his small-town Baptist Church on Sundays where I learned *gratitude and giving* habits, combining redeemed human nature and the restored natural world. Grandpa showed awe and respect for God and for the land.

Do you have a few companions with whom to travel the wild places?

Discovery

> *Goals for experiencing mountains like Colorado's fourteeners are as numerous as the people who climb them. Some people are content just to look at the fourteeners. Some people are excited if they manage to climb one. Many are content climbing the easier ones and just gaze at the harder ones. Choose your list and finish each climb wanting more. Never lose your spirit of discovery! (Roach)*[26]

Climbing Colorado fourteeners began for me in 1999 when my dad and I climbed Mt. Elbert. It is the highest peak in Colorado and has a Class 1 trail all the way to the summit at 14,433 feet. The North Mount Elbert Trailhead is at 10,050 feet and rises 4400 vertical feet over 4.5 miles to the top. The nine-mile roundtrip took dad about 11 hours to complete at dad's age of 81. *Develop your spirit of discovery!*

I never set a goal of climbing all the Colorado fourteeners. The list I referenced contained 54 mountain peaks over 14,000 feet and today usually includes a total of 58 peaks. There are several different lists. At last count I now have summited 50 different fourteeners and have repeated some of my favorites with family members over the last 25 years. *Never lose your spirit of discovery!*

Backpacking and climbing in Colorado has been about much more than "bagging" peaks. We camped in remote wilderness areas with names such as: Halfmoon and East Cross Creek; Needle Creek and Chicago Basin. We've seen pristine wilderness with quiet alpine lakes and apocalyptic lightning storms and wildlife sightings.

Be humbled by wilderness. Discover the natural world.

Nature

For many people in the world, the landscape before us would be foreboding. For us, it had been a gradual ascent from the unknown into the familiar. Beyond the last villages we no longer saw strange human alterings of the scene, but rather the workings of nature common to all the world's alpine areas: glaciers, rivers, clouds, granite, blue sky, raindrops, wildlife, and friends who shared our passions. We were home again. (Rowell)

I can hear the voices now saying, "that's your thing but it's not mine." I understand. As I got immersed in grad school, doctoral work, and a career in higher education, I drifted away from regular time in nature. But I know a medical doctor who stays rooted and connected in her garden, finding "simplicity and contentment digging in the dirt." A friend of mine has a cabin getaway near a forest on "the edge of the wilderness."

Human nature is designed to thrive in physical nature and natural environments. Restoring our nature has a dual meaning: to redeem human nature and to restore the natural world. God spoke: "Earth, generate life! Every sort and kind: cattle and reptiles and wild animals- all kinds.

God created human beings, reflecting God's nature, and told them to be responsible for every living thing on the Earth." (Genesis 1:28)

Blue Zones are regions in the world where people are claimed to live longer than average, even to 100 years. The concept resulted from demographic work published by Michel Poulain in 2004. Longevity was attributed to the practice of a traditional lifestyle, regular physical activity beyond the age of 80, family and community support for elders, and consuming locally produced food.

Wendell Berry writes that we have an environmental crisis because we have consented to an economy in which by eating, drinking, working, resting, traveling, and enjoying ourselves we are destroying the natural, the God-given, world. *Restore Your Nature and the Natural World!*

Highpoints

Whether your goal is to reach the highpoint of your state or the highpoint of each of the fifty states, it is a goal shared by many across the United States. You may be an experienced mountaineer accepting challenges on Denali or Gannett Peak, a veteran hiker scaling the slopes of Guadalupe Peak or an automobile explorer driving the roads of Mount Mitchell. Whatever your level of skill and interest, the highpoints of the U.S. offer a diversity of experiences. (Holmes)[27]

Having accepted the challenge of the 50 Peaks, I was more than a little surprised to find that so many state highpoints involved only a long drive from my home in Texas. Dividing the state highpoints into four regions: the South (13), the Northeast (12), the Midwest (12), and the West (13), allowed me to combine multiple peaks on a long road-trip. Those in the South and Midwest regions were all easy hikes or drive-ups. Three climbs in the Northeast region can be Class 2 hikes—Vermont, Maine, and New Hampshire.

RIVERS, HIGHPOINTS

The highpoints of the thirteen western states are distinct mountains, and taller peaks from Mt. Hood at 11,239 feet to Mt. McKinley (Denali) at 20,320 feet. Five of the 13 are strenuous day hikes, two require an overnight camp, three are multi-day backpacks into remote wilderness, two are both heavily glaciated volcanoes which require climbing skills and gear, and one is the highest mountain in North America in a class by itself, undertaken only by experienced alpinists.

Like those who have hiked the Appalachian Trail or the Pacific Coast Trail, these endeavors require endurance and perseverance and pain. *By climbing we find we can do hard things and perseverance produces hope. That's a high point.*

Faith

"I could never go into the wilderness to hike or to camp and I would never go alone. I would be scared to death." These remarks from a woman that I know followed several of my stories about my solo climbs in the backcountry. I sensed fear in her response and in her tone of voice. We live in a culture of fear—fear of the unknown, fear of the other, fear of failure, fear of death, fear of never being enough, on and on.

Faith and unbelief are not opposites, faith and fear are. Bruce Larson described FEAR as False Evidence Appearing Real. We taught all three daughters that we are not people of fear, we are people of faith. What is faith? Certainly, faith is a belief in a Higher Being. My friend and Jesuit priest Rick Ganz says that "faith is a highly developed capacity for adventure." Faith is risk and risk-taking requires faith. *Step out on faith.*

High in the California Sierras on a climb of the East Face of Mt. Whitney, our AAI guide Joey saw some fear in me and said," Tom, you look a little nervous." As we inched along a narrow stretch of rock ledge with a steep precipice dropping thousands of feet below us, I replied, "When I look down it is a long drop." Joey said, "Don't look down. Look where you want to step and don't look where you don't want to step."

I have carried that mountain wisdom in my heart and in my mind with me ever since! Fear is a lack of focus. Faith is a seed in human nature that is meant to grow. We went on to summit Mt. Whitney, the highest mountain in the continental U.S. at 14,500 feet. We descended the same vertical route down to Upper Boy

Scout Lake. I will never forget that climb and I will never forget: *Faith is a highly developed capacity for adventure.*

Resistance

You must find your own way in life. Two things have helped me: (1) journeys into the mountains and wilderness; (2) the companions who have joined me in exploration. Thanks to my family, friends, and strangers for being my hiking and climbing partners. We've had a few setbacks and many memorable adventures. Never Stop Exploring!

In *Upon That Mountain,* Eric Shipton points out that "Mountain climbing has its roots in mountain exploration."[28] Shipton's focus was shifting away from a chief interest in climbing peaks. He had spent four months on Everest with a large travelling community attempting to summit. Gradually, he returned to his early feeling for exploring mountains rather than bagging peaks, influenced by a fellow explorer.

Pay attention to those experiences that alienate you from yourself. Find your own way in your wilderness wanderings. I used a guide on several mountains—Rainier, Hood, Kilimanjaro, Mt. Kenya, the East Face of Mt. Whitney—and I'm glad I did. But guided climbing leads to a guided mentality. As we move on in life we need to test our skills.

A technique for running, as well as other physical activities, that will test you is called resistance training. Runners, for example, do repeats on a 200-meter hill or incline to build endurance. A test of my mountain exploration skills was solo climbing. My solo climbs included some state highpoints like Granite Peak in Montana and Mount Katahdin in Maine. I climbed alone on Mt. Shasta in the Cascades and Mount Lyell in Yosemite and a dozen or so Colorado Fourteeners.

Resistance tests our skills, our resolve, and our faith.

Base Camp

Base Camp is not a military installation for basic training nor is it a low-elevation beginner's encampment. The term Base Camp in mountaineering refers to rudimentary campsites used by climbers during their ascents and descents. A base camp is a place climbers leave from and return to on the mountain. It is a place to re-supply and to rest, acclimating to higher altitudes or waiting out nasty weather.

Our base camp on Aconcagua, Plaza de Mulas, was at 14,400 feet in the Andes Mountains of Argentina. There are two base camps on Mount Everest on opposite sides of the mountain: South Base Camp in Nepal at an altitude of 17,598 feet while North Base Camp in China at 16,900 feet. Shawn and I set up a base camp at the Chicago Basin in the Weminuche Wilderness of the San Juan Mountains to create a staging site for four peaks—Eolus, North Eolus, Windom, and Sunlight.

Base Camp on any big mountain is present because the expeditions involve weeks or months, making it a place of provision during the climbing season. It is a location for relative safety and can be a place for gaining physical strength and sustenance for the challenge ahead. Loads are carried up the mountain to provision base camp. Supplies are then moved to higher camps as the climbers ascend.

Drawing a parallel with life, the prayer room is a spiritual person's base camp. It is a place of supernatural provision and solace. Rightly viewed, it is the place we depart from each morning and return to each evening. We enter the day with the inner strength gained there and end the day in a quiet place to be renewed.

Base Camp is a transfer station on the mountain of life.

Alpine DNA

My love of mountains comes naturally from my family DNA. Mom was born under a tree on the east side of the Sandia Mountains near Edgewood, New Mexico. Here are some lines from my poem *The Land of Enchantment* remembering her:

> *So close to your mother, So close to the earth*
> *You know a Greater Spirit was there, witnessing your birth.*
> *So, your mountain streams flow through my blood . . .*

My dad was born in a small central Texas town and lived in northern New Mexico when he was a child. Here are a few lines from my poem Father Sky (Son's Prayer) honoring him:

> *Father Sky, teach us to fly, to reach high, to laugh and cry,*
> *Deep blue eyes by day, sparkle white by night . . .*
> *Let us feel the golden sun and run hand in hand,*
> *With the man in the moon.*

Since I was child, I've had this picture in my mind of a small log cabin in the mountains sitting beside a mountain stream and a column of smoke rising from the rock chimney. I don't know if it was just a childhood dream, or a grown-up idea of a peaceful place surrounded by tall mountains of rock and snow. I've never found that place on my hiking trips.

I have found pristine mountain streams in alpine meadows to renew my soul. Human nature can be restored by natural environments and natural environments can be respected and protected by the best of humanity.

You let me rest in meadows of green grass, by streams of peaceful water. It's in my DNA. It's within human nature.

Design

Every September I take a flyfishing trip to Colorado with 14–15 men who share the vocation of Christian camping. Many of these guys had a career as a Camp Director. In his book *Blueprints*, Dan Bolin, writes: "Few tools in God's toolbox are as effective as Christian camping. So, why does it work? Maybe God built us to be campers! Maybe the more we align ourselves with God's design, the more we become aware of God's glory seen in creation."[29]

I've spent many weeks at Christian Camps from Family Camp every August in Ceta Canyon, Texas, to Spiritual Retreats at Redwood Christian Park near Boulder Creek, California. A dominant memory of all those experiences has been time outdoors exploring nature. Gazing up at giant redwood trees, hiking to the waterfalls, swimming in the lakes, running dirt trails, and walking with old and new friends enriches indoor lectures. These people are my climbing companions!

I do remember a few talks and mountain lessons from attending Christian Camp. When Jesus saw his ministry drawing huge crowds, he climbed a mountain. Those who were his apprentices climbed with him. Arriving at a quiet place, he sat down and taught his climbing companions. This is what he said on the mountain:

> "You're blessed when you're at the end of your rope . . .
> You're blessed when you feel you've lost what is most dear . . .
> You're blessed when you're content with just who you are . . .
> You're blessed when you've worked up an appetite for God . . .
> You're blessed when you care . . .

You're blessed when you can show people how to cooperate. You're blessed when you get your inner world put right . . . "
(Matthew 5 MSG)

Journey

The journey is not to just keep going to new places, making the trip a vacation or travelogue. We have to return to where we started and know it in a new way and do life in a new way. By denying their pain and avoiding the necessary falling, many have kept themselves from their own spiritual journeys and depths—and therefore have been kept from their own spiritual heights. (Rohr)[30]

Climbing in the Wind River Range of Wyoming with climbing partners Shawn and Kent, I took a couple of "necessary falls." Descending on snow from Gannett Peak above Gooseneck Glacier, I lost my concentration kicking steps in snow on a vertical section. I didn't fall far but it hurt my pride. Around day six or seven, we were descending narrow trails near Island Lake and one of my trekking poles ricocheted off a rock causing my legs to tangle. I fell on my face and my sunglasses cut my head above my right eye.

I've never used trekking poles again. I began to do life (and hiking) in a new way. But the larger life lesson is this: Get up every day, keep climbing mountains, and go for the heights with a few trusted companions. Journey with those who know God and then:

"You are blessed when there is more of God around you . . .
You are blessed when you are embraced by God's love . . .
You are blessed when you are cared for . . .
You are blessed when you value what can't be bought . . .
You are blessed when you find your place in God's family . . .
You are blessed when you can see God in the outside world."
(Matthew 5 MSG)

May your children and grandchildren pursue these values too. Take the journey! Let's keep Restoring Our Nature.

STREAMS

a body of running water flowing on the earth

Trust

In August 2013, my climbing partner Shawn and I set out to climb at least nine Colorado 14ers in the Sawatch Range over seven days, maybe more. One of them, in particular, La Plata Peak, was a top priority. The previous year, in bluebird September weather, our first attempt at this relatively easy peak failed. Three of us were busy talking as we hiked, and we missed a turn, ending on top of an unnamed peak.

We made the summit in 2013 just as midday storms exploded, bombarding us with blowing rain, snow pellets, hailstones, and lightning flashes. It reminded me of a story entitled "the wind ran out of breath," when a huge storm came up with fierce winds threatening to sink a boat on the Sea of Galilee. This and other Biblical stories like it have produced "a storm theology" among some believers.

Simply put: You are just coming out of a storm in your life, you are in a storm, or one is coming soon. I know that storms and bad things happen in life. Rivers flood, people drown; snow slabs avalanche, people die; lightning strikes, people lose. Storms are real, and they test our faith.

One of my spiritual mentors, though very theologically astute, never developed a systematic theology. He developed instead what we call a Christology, focused on "the unsearchable riches of Christ." We abide in Christ. We do not have to defeat the storm. We simply remain in Him who has defeated the storm. Accept His victory.

When he calmed the storm in the above-mentioned story, his climbing companions and closest followers asked themselves, "Who is this, anyway, that even the wind and the sea obey"?

It's within our nature to trust God. That is the whole truth. God in our inner stances is greater than our circumstances!

Transformation

One of our first backpacking adventures was a three-week expedition through Yellowstone National Park and the Teton Range in Wyoming. The trip was organized and led by a Geology professor from Texas with a group of 21 students. As we finally arrived near Jackson Hole, we were "transformed" by the breathtaking view of the Grand Tetons.

"Transformed" is a great word, typically overused and misused in our culture. "A college education will transform your life." "Travel is transformational." "That movie transformed my life." Education, travel, or a great movie are formational— they can shape who you are as a person or even change the direction of your life. Transformation is more than change.

As our backpacking team prepared to spend nine days in the Wyoming and Idaho backcountry, we made one last stop at the Chapel of the Transfiguration which is a tiny log cabin church with a nature-inspired view of the mountains there. Its name is a reference to an event described in the New Covenant where Jesus appears in his divine nature and becomes radiant in glory upon a mountain, likely Mount Tabor.

Transfiguration and transformation point to a deeper meaning. Jesus was fully human and fully divine. On Mount Tabor, his divine nature *moved across* his human nature revealing clearly and radiantly his true form. When we humans experience transformation, the Spirit of God (the divine nature) *moves across* our human soul and re-forms it. We enter the divine nature.

God came down so that we could go up. We meet on the mountain.

Resources

There are human resources and natural resources, external resources and internal resources, food resources and water resources, latent resources and developed resources. Wildlands, wilderness, and mountains are resources set aside for preservation and protection from development. *With dollars in your eyes, some developer's disguise, your money is not welcome here.*

God's resources are infinite and eternal. Mankind's resources are finite and temporal. The brief definition of economics is stated as "limited resources and unlimited human wants." The market system allocates and rations resources through the pricing mechanism. The command system controls resources through government ownership of production and distribution. Wilderness is a resource free of ownership.

Do you know the difference between a for-profit organization (sole proprietor, partnership, corporation) and a nonprofit organization (NPO or NGO)? *It is not profit; it is ownership.* No one owns a nonprofit organization. No one owns a national forest, the national parks, the wilderness, or the mountains. They are not resources to exploit.

There is a story of an Egyptian servant and her son who was perishing without water. As the story tells quite simply, "God opened her eyes, and she saw a well." It was enough water to save their lives. There are amazing resources in your life that you may miss if you don't let God touch your eyes.

Go to the wilderness and the mountains. You will find inner resources. Accept the quickening touch of God on the eyes of your imagination.

Truth

If the city is a metaphor for certainty and belonging, then the wilderness is for questions and truth. —**Sarah Bessey**, *Field Notes.*[31]

What is certainty and what is belonging? We go to the desert and the wilderness with our questions, not seeking answers but receiving them in the truth of wild places. We reconnect with Nature. We reconnect with the Earth in the mountains and forests that God created. We hike rugged trails, climb beyond the mountain paths, and find majestic views. We belong. Our souls need this.

Last April I was planning my daily hike in the Sandia Mountains while in Albuquerque, New Mexico. After doing our two-mile morning walk at the Los Poblanos Open Fields with two kids from our condos, one asked to go with me on my daily four-mile hike up in the mountains. We've known the three kids for over four years, so I reluctantly agreed to allow the fifteen-year-old to join me on a challenging hike.

My teenage hiking partner was a girl whose families are from the San Felipe and Santo Domingo Pueblos. At about 8000 feet up the Piedra Lisa Trail, we noticed a cane cholla cactus perfectly shaped like a cross. Since we were in the middle of Holy Week, we talked about the Cross, Good Friday, and Easter. She told me about her Pueblo Feast days on Easter.

You could say the majestic views and clear mountain air were good for the soul and you would be right. The physical climb was challenging for Carol, moving slowly at altitude and resting frequently. The only question she spoke out loud was "how does an old guy like you climb faster than me?"

I hoped that her heart and mind would receive silent answers to her unspoken questions. We all have existential questions.

Jesus will make a way where there is no way, Jesus will be the truth when nothing seems true, and Jesus will be full of life when you are empty. He stands at the door and knocks.

Reset

One of the shepherds who maintains a careful watch for the spiritual needs of all the members of our flock encourages the annual "Reset." Like an annual physical exam, the Reset is a regular spiritual exam, often at the beginning of the school year or the calendar year. The actual word *pastor* is derived from a Latin word meaning "shepherd." Jesus called himself the "Good Shepherd."

I annually do a "Mountain Reset." Where am I going this year? Who is going with me? What resources will I need? For example, my 2024 Mountain Goals were: June—Hiking Sandia trails; July—Climbing Wheeler Peak with Wiley family; August—Arkansas hikes; September— Climb Blanca Peak and Humboldt Peak, Colorado, with Shawn; September—Climb Cabezon Peak and Manzano Peak in New Mexico.

My "Life Reset" in the last five years has focused on writing and publishing, a transition to becoming an author. Envisioning and writing something I call "The Mountain Series" has produced three books: *Retreat Upward: A Mountain Pathway for the Soul*; *Moving Mountains: Paying Attention to Weather and Climate*; and *Mountain Streams: Restoring Our Nature*. Writing is hard work.

Transitioning out of public speaking and board training, I continue to use organized plans and personalized structures to communicate in writing what "regular resets" provide for purpose-driven living. What I am now communicating in my written articles and books is the accumulation of my teaching and training experiences.

I developed and wrote The Summit Series which contains three presentations:

- Ascend 1—Making the Most of Your Workday
- Ascend 2—Making the Most of Your Life
- Ascend 3—Making the Most of Your History/Legacy

Are you willing to hit 'Reset'? Ask God to lead you. Reset your workday, reset your life, reset your legacy.

Breath

The breath of Life is a gift, something you receive. The ability to breathe at altitude is acquired.

High altitude hiking and climbing brings with it beautiful scenery and what feels like thinner air. The physical effort involved in simply walking leaves you struggling for breath or feeling out-of-breath. Your body increases your respiration rate in an effort to bring in more oxygen. The reason you have difficulty breathing at high altitudes is that the barometric pressure decreases as you ascend.

The International Society for Mountain Medicine recognizes three altitude regions which reflect the lowered amount of oxygen in the atmosphere due to lower barometric pressure:

- High altitude = 4900—11500 feet (1500—3500 meters)
- Very high altitude = 11500–18000 feet (3500—5500m)
- Extreme altitude = above 18000 feet (above 5500m)

Travel in each of these altitude regions can lead to medical problems, from the mild symptoms of acute mountain sickness (AMS) to the potentially fatal high-altitude pulmonary edema (HAPE) and high-altitude cerebral edema (HACE).

My climbing experience in extreme altitude has included Mt. Kilimanjaro (19,341 ft.) and Mt. Aconcagua (22,800 ft). At times I have lived at altitudes of 4000–5000 feet, and I usually adapt to higher regions easily with acclimatization. Acute mountain sickness or high-altitude edema can strike anyone at any time. I drink plenty of water before I feel thirst and I acclimate slowly as I begin to ascend.

Sometimes life at sea level or life in our urban busyness leaves us "out-of-breath." Work and play cause us to live alienated from the natural world. Family vacations drain our energy and bank account. Our pace of life creates illness and lowered immune systems. Doctors at John Hopkins Hospital have learned that many diseases are passed along to our bodies from our minds and emotions.

God gives breath to the people on earth and the Spirit to those walking in it.

Reconciliation

In my book, *Moving Mountains*, I write, "Our noisy and busy urban lives cause us to live alienated from the natural world and from ourselves. Mountains awaken us to what is real and essential."[32] We need to reconcile humans and nature. The restoration of friendly relations is variously called reconciling, reuniting, or reunion of estranged groups or individuals. And it also applies to our relationship with land and wilderness.

Aldo Leopold saw a progression of ethical sensitivity from interpersonal relationships (between individuals), linked to relationships to society and the common good, and linked to relationships with the land. These linkages lead to a steady decrease or reduction of human actions based on expediency, conquest, and self-interest. He rejected utilitarianism.

During my high school years, I became an Eagle Scout, an Explorer, and a member of the Order of the Arrow, committed to the protection and preservation of our national forests, national parks, and mountain wilderness areas. To fulfill this lifetime oath, I have hiked or camped in most of America's sixty-three national parks. For most people these experiences are remote from everyday life.

What is the value of thinking or reading about wilderness? The contemplation of wild places opens us to a sense of the sacred in our homes and communities. We need to look up to the heights and reflect on the world around us and on the God who made us. We need to be reconciled with God because our relationship with Him is neglected at best, or worse, is broken.

The message of reuniting is simple: "Be reconciled to God." Our relationship with God can be restored. "One plants, one waters, and God brings growth." Our human nature and our natural world are sacred. Start having a conversation with God.

Navigation

Hikers and climbers in the great mountain ranges will value this definition of navigation—"the process or activity of accurately ascertaining one's position by planning and following a route." Navigating is a constant process of staying on or returning to the route. From wilderness maps to GPS devices to navigating by the stars, explorers of the natural world rely on this active skill of monitoring and course-correcting our movements.

We are positional people. We like to know where we are. In the backcountry we "read" the position of the sun in the day and the location of stars and constellations at night. Like ships on the ocean or planes in the skies, we move from one place to another by simple or sophisticated navigational tools. What is our position?

Grace is the unmerited favor of God. Or "God's love set free." There is a sharp distinction drawn in Scripture between what God has done for us by grace, and how we are to live in view of this fact. The divine order reveals to humans the sequence involved: (1) sit still and learn your position and (2) live a life and move through it, consistent with your position. The Christian life is becoming what you already are positionally.

I once heard a former pro football player and then college head coach give his faith testimony and position in life. As a defensive linebacker with the Washington Redskins, he knew well his position on the team and how to play it. At the end of that career, he heard God say "you're out of position. I'm moving you to a new position as a head coach." He called it God's GPS.

Navigation is essential and accurate when you know your position. When you depend on God, you acknowledge your spiritual poverty; you acknowledge His significance. Locate yourself in God.

Discipline

Markings, a book by and about Dag Hammarskjold, was published after his death in a plane crash while he was negotiating a ceasefire agreement. He was a Swedish economist and diplomat who served as the second Secretary General of the United Nations from 1953 to 1961.

The reader of *Markings* may well be surprised by what the book does not contain—that Dag Hammarskjold did not make a single direct reference to his career as an international civil servant, to the important persons he met, or the historical events of his time in which he played an important role.

Integrity is our commitment to adhere to the truth, and it describes the nature of discipline in Hammarskjold's life. A disciplined life contains these qualities: desire, integrity, intentionality, study, commitment, prayer, listening, rest, nutrition, and exercise. "Discipline" sounds harsh but the practice of these ten qualities will produce the freedom to really live well.

The nature of discipline is truly about personal discovery. My core values include family, friendships, and faith in God. I discovered from that foundation that I love the four "silent sports" of kayaking, flyfishing, trail running, and alpine mountaineering. It is the desire of my heart to practice these sports. Desire produces discipline. I grew up near the Rocky Mountains and that alone may explain my passion for hiking and climbing in the mountains or fishing a trout stream.

Peeling back the layers of my desire, I find my enjoyment of the outdoors and my attraction to the pristine beauty of nature and wilderness. I love kayaking on the mountain lake in the early morning, observing the deer drinking at the water's edge and the beaver building its dam to protect themselves from predators. I also love to climb a rock wall.

It is the nature of discipline to risk, to step out on faith.

Resilience

It is not your love that will sustain your commitment. It is your commitment that will sustain your love.

The quote above is one I attribute to one of the ten men who have formed my "band of brothers" for over 35 years. We get together at least once a year to deepen our friendships and take trusted counsel from one another. They are committed to me, and I am committed to them. Commitment is the heart of discipline. The word resilience expresses the meaning of commitment better than oath, vow, or promise.

Resilience is faithfulness. It describes the prepared condition of both a disciplined body and a disciplined mind. *Resilient people are committed to finishing strong.*[33] Commitment and resilience are built one challenge at a time. Last summer my daughter and her two sons had a desire to climb Wheeler Peak, New Mexico's highest mountain, with me. They met the "resilience challenge" at ages 7 and 11.

My dad became a distance runner in his mid-fifties. He began to run laps at the local track in summer and inside the gym in winter. The habit stuck and thirteen years later he ran the NYC Marathon in under five hours at 68 years of age. He established an annual 5K race that celebrated a 40-year streak in his small town. Dad ran and jogged daily until he was 90 and walked daily until his death at 96 years of age.

That is commitment! I would call it resilience. This kind of resilience—in daily exercise, in marriage, in business, and in life—is the heart of discipline. And, by the way, *resilience produces solid friendships. Dad had lots of friends.*

5.

To the Destination

Brooks, Creeks, Rivers and Streams represent many things in literature and writing. Most frequently, they symbolize a path or a journey from a source in the mountains to a destination. The mouth of a river is its destination—the lake, the inland sea, or the ocean. Sometimes that destination is known. Other times, it is a mystery. Great indeed, we confess, is the mystery of God. Follow the mystery. It is the way we were created to live.

The term 'mystery' occurs as many as 43 times in the Bible, most often in the New Covenant. Holy Scripture is filled with hidden truths, profound questions, and open secrets that invite curiosity and contemplation. Accepting the concept of mystery allows us to grasp the complexities of faith and the divine nature of God. We must reflect on the fact that not all things are entirely revealed to us.

Have you ever wondered where a river begins and then explored the mystery in person? I never thought much about the source and the destination of the Arkansas River until we lived in Arkansas. I traced the river's origin on a map in reverse from Arkansas to Oklahoma and then Kansas and up into the mountains of Colorado.

Mountain Streams

One year I hiked to the source of the Arkansas River just east of Leadville, Colorado, in the Sawatch Mountains. It flows 1469 miles to its destination, converging with the Mississippi River near Napoleon, Arkansas. The journey it takes from a tiny spring to a mighty river flowing to the Gulf of Mexico is still filled with mystery and questions.

A river flowed out of Eden to water the garden, and there it divided and became four rivers. The symbolism of the river is that God causes the agricultural abundance of His creation. The four rivers were "branch streams" likely referring to ancient waterways. Then the Lord God took the man and put him into the garden of Eden to cultivate it and keep it.

All creation is the backdrop or stage for God's love affair with created mankind. Fallen mankind has assaulted the natural environment with selfish abandon. Not only are we reaping the result of pollution and resource exploitation, but our children and grandchildren will reap even more severe, non-reversible effects. This quote is from *The Canon of Westminster* by Edward Carpenter:

> Man's relentless assault, in a global context, upon the universe around him—that is on God's creation—is an attack on the air which he pollutes; the natural waterways which he befouls; the soil which he poisons; the forests which he hews down, heedless of the long-term effects of this wanton destruction. Scant regard is paid to any balance of nature and consequently little sense of responsibility for what one generation owes to another.[34]

Mountain Streams: Restoring Our Nature was written to encourage us to live as stewards of God's creation. We are bound to this natural order. Humankind has abused God's gift of nature as we have all the other good gifts of God, including the divine nature of redeemed humans. God is moving our world to a historical nexus. Creation will be redeemed. Begin to participate in the life of God.

Live in the way God designed humans to live and protect the natural world and wilderness places by the way we live.

Endnotes

1. Jones, E. Stanley. *A Song of Ascents*. Nashville: Abingdon, 1968.
2. Leopold, Aldo. *A Sand County Almanac*. Oxford: Oxford University Press, 1949.
3. Peterson, Eugene. *The Message*. Colorado Springs, CO: NavPress, 2002.
4. Following quotes from Jones, E. Stanley. *A Song of Ascents*. Nashville: Abingdon, 1968.
5. Leopold, Aldo. *A Sand County Almanac*. Oxford: Oxford University Press, 1949.
6. Nisbett, Richard A. "Where We Explore." LinkedIn post: Aldo Leopold Foundation, 2025.
7. Following quotes drawn from Aldo Leopold. *A Sand County Almanac*. Oxford: Oxford University Press, 1949.
8. Leopold, Aldo. *A Sand County Almanac*. Oxford: Oxford University Press, 1949.
9. Farjeon, Eleanor. Morning Has Broken. Wikipedia, Songs of Praise, 1931.
10. Matthiessen, Peter. *The Snow Leopard*. New York: Viking Press, 1978.
11. Chesterton, G. K. *Quotes*. Chicago: Encyclopedia Britannica, 2025.
12. Chouinard, Yvon. *Let My People Go Surfing*. New York: Penguin Books, 2005.
13. Sutterfield, Ragan. *Wendell Berry and the Given Life*, Cincinnati, Ohio: Franciscan Media, 2017.
14. Sutterfield, Ragan. *Wendell Berry and the Given Life*, Cincinnati, Ohio: Franciscan Media, 2017.
15. Merton, Thomas. *The Wisdom of the Desert*. New York: New Directions Publishing, 1970.
16. Fuchs, V.E. Quoted by Tom Griffiths, *Slicing the Silence,* London: Harvard University Press, 2007.
17. Nichols, John. *If Mountains Die*, New York: W.W. Norton & Company, 1994.
18. Brokaw, Tom. Quoted in his Foreword, *Galen Rowell: A Retrospective,*

Endnotes

San Francisco: Sierra Club Books, 2006.

19. Bernbaum, Edwin. *Sacred Mountains of the World*, Cambridge, UK: Cambridge University Press, 2022.

20. Five Benefits of Mountains. Food and Agriculture Organization of the United Nations, FAO, 2024.

21. Perrin, Jim. *Shipton & Tilman: The Great Decade of Himalayan Exploration*, London: Random House, 2013.

22. Perrin, Jim. *Shipton & Tilman: The Great Decade of Himalayan Exploration*, London: Random House, 2013.

23. Beales, Finn, Curator. *Let's Get Lost*. London: White Lion, 2021.

24. Sierra Club Books Editors. *Galen Rowell: A Retrospective*. San Francisco: Sierra Club Books, 2006.

25. Ridgeway, Rick. *Seven Summits*. New York: Warner Books, 1986.

26. Roach, Gerry. *Colorado's Fourteeners*, 2nd edition, Golden, CO: Fulcrum Publishing, 1999.

27. Holmes, Don. *Highpoints of the United States: A Guide to the Fifty State Summits*. Salt Lake City: The University of Utah Press, 2000.

28. Shipton, Eric. *Upon That Mountain*. Sheffield, UK: Vertebrate Digital, 2015.

29. Bolin, Dan. *Blueprints*. Arlington, VA: RIF Publishing, 2022.

30. Rohr, Richard. *Richard Rohr's Daily Meditations*, Albuquerque: Center for Action and Contemplation, 2025.

31. Bessey, Sarah. *Field Notes for the Wilderness*. New York: Convergent Books Imprint of Random House, 2024

32. Nisbett, Thomas. *Moving Mountains: Paying Attention to Weather and Climate*. Eugene, OR: Resource Publications, 2025.

33. McDonald, Gordon. *A Resilient Life*. Nashville: Thomas Nelson, 2006.

34. Carpenter, Edward. *The Canon of Westminster*. London: Westminster Abbey, 1896.

Mountain Streams Playlist

"Another Shore" – Liz Story
"Babbling Brook" – Anthony Phillips
"Behind the Waterfall" – David Lanz and Paul Speer
"Crossing Waters" – Stanton Lanier
"Crow River Waltz" – Leo Kottke
"Currents" – Dave Beegle
"Hunter Creek" – Lynn Patrick
"Light of the Water" – David Arkenstone
"Orinoco Flow" – Enya
"Reflections" – Michael Mucklow
"River Crossing" – David Arkenstone
"River of Peace" – Dave Beegle
"Sacred Mountain" – Stanton Lanier
"So Flows the Current" – Patrick O'Hearn
"Spring Creek" – George Winston
"The Sun in the Stream" – Enya
"The Transcendent Mountain" – Antione Dufour
"Water Blessing" – Josh Jaffe and Jim 'Kimo' West
"Water Caves" – Liz Story
"Water of Life" – David Arkenstone
"What Can Be" – Lance Takamiya
"Wild River" – David Arkenstone

www.ingramcontent.com/pod-product-compliance
Lightning Source LLC
Chambersburg PA
CBHW072159160426
43197CB00012B/2450